SCRIPTURE

God's Word for Contemporary Christians

JOHN STOTT

with Scott Hotaling

6 studies
for individuals or groups

CHRISTIAN BASICS BIBLE STUDIES

With Guidelines for
Leaders & Study Notes
NIV Text Included

INTERVARSITY PRESS
DOWNERS GROVE, ILLINOIS, USA
LEICESTER, ENGLAND

InterVarsity Press
P.O. Box 1400, Downers Grove, IL 60515, USA
38 De Montfort Street, Leicester LE1 7GP, England

©1994 by John Stott

InterVarsity Press®, U.S.A., is the book-publishing division of InterVarsity Christian Fellowship®, a student movement active on campus at hundreds of universities, colleges and schools of nursing in the United States of America, and a member movement of the International Fellowship of Evangelical Students. For information about local and regional activities, write Public Relations Dept., InterVarsity Christian Fellowship, 6400 Schroeder Rd., P.O. Box 7895, Madison, WI 53707-7895.

Inter-Varsity Press, England, is the book-publishing division of the Universities and Colleges Christian Fellowship (formerly the Inter-Varsity Fellowship), a student movement linking Christian Unions in universities and colleges throughout the United Kingdom and the Republic of Ireland, and a member movement of the International Fellowship of Evangelical Students. For information about local and national activities write to UCCF, 38 De Montfort Street, Leicester LE1 7GP.

This study guide is based on and adapts material from The Contemporary Christian *©1992 by John R. W. Stott.*

Some material in study one and its notes was originally published in Favorite Psalms *by John R. W. Stott (Chicago: Moody Press, 1988).*

Some material in studies three and five and their notes was originally published in The Message of 2 Timothy *by John R. W. Stott (Downers Grove, Ill.: InterVarsity Press, 1973).*

Some material in study four was originally published in Declare His Glory, "The Two Comings of Christ" *by John R. W. Stott (Downers Grove, Ill.: InterVarsity Press, 1971).*

Cover photograph: Michael Goss
Cover background: Cowgirl Stock Photography ©1991

USA ISBN 0-8308-2001-9
UK ISBN 0-85111-344-3

Printed in the United States of America

15	14	13	12	11	10	9	8	7	6	5	4	3	2	1

| 04 | 03 | 02 | 01 | 00 | 99 | 98 | 97 | 96 | 95 | 94 |

Getting the Most Out of Christian Basics Bible Studies

The essentials of our faith: knowing Christ, understanding Scripture, following Jesus in all areas of life, learning how to pray in the midst of a busy life, understanding how our faith is lived out at work, experiencing true worship, developing Christian character, and setting priorities that are godly. These are the topics in this series designed to help you become a more mature believer.

What Kind of Guide Is This?

The studies are not designed to merely tell you what one person thinks. Instead, through inductive study, they will help you discover for yourself what Scripture is saying. Each study deals with a particular passage—rather than jumping around the Bible—so that you can really delve into the author's meaning in that context.

The studies ask three different kinds of questions. *Observation* questions help you to understand the content of the passage by asking about the basic facts: who, what, when, where and how. *Interpretation* questions delve into the meaning of the passage. *Application* questions help you discover its implications for growing in Christ. These three keys unlock the treasures of the biblical writings and help you live them out.

This is a thought-provoking guide. Each question assumes a variety of answers. Many questions do not have "right" answers, particularly questions that aim at meaning or application. Instead, the questions should inspire users to explore the passage more thoroughly.

This study guide is flexible. You can use it for individual study, but it is also great for a variety of groups—student, professional, neighborhood or church groups. Each study takes about forty-five minutes in a group setting or thirty minutes in personal study.

How They're Put Together

Each study is composed of four sections: opening paragraphs and questions to help you get into the topic, the NIV text and questions that invite study of the passage, questions to help you apply what you have learned, and a suggestion for prayer.

The workbook format provides space for writing a response to each question. This format is ideal for personal study and allows group members to prepare in advance for the discussion and/or write down notes during the study. This space can form a permanent record of your thoughts and spiritual progress.

At the back of the guide are study notes which may be useful for leaders or for individuals. These notes do not give "the answers," but they do provide additional background information on certain questions to help you through the difficult spots.

The "Guidelines for Leaders" section describes how to lead a group discussion, gives helpful tips on group dynamics and suggests ways to deal with problems which may arise during the discussion. With such helps, someone with little or no experience can lead an effective group study.

Suggestions for Individual Study

1. If you have not read the book or booklet suggested in the "further reading" section, you may want to read the portion suggested before you begin your study.

2. Read the introduction. Consider the opening questions and note your responses.

3. Pray, asking God to speak to you from his Word about this particular topic.

4. Read the passage reproduced for you in the New International Version. You may wish to mark phrases that seem important. Note in the margin any questions that come to your mind as you read.

5. Use the questions from the study guide to more thoroughly examine the passage. Note your findings in the space provided. After you have made your own notes, read the corresponding study notes in the back of the book for further insights.

6. Reread the entire passage, making further notes about its general principles and about the way you intend to use them.

7. Move to the "commit" section. Spend time prayerfully considering what the passage has to say specifically to your life.

8. Read the suggestion for prayer. Speak to God about insights you have gained. Tell him of any desires you have for specific growth. Ask him to help you as you attempt to live out the principles described in that passage.

Suggestions for Members of a Group Study

Joining a Bible study group can be a great avenue to spiritual growth. Here are a few guidelines that will help you as you participate in the studies in this guide.

1. These studies focus on a particular passage of Scripture—in depth. Only rarely should you refer to other portions of the Bible, and then only at the request of the leader. Of course, the Bible is internally consistent. Other good forms of study draw on that consistency, but inductive Bible study sticks with a single passage and works on it in depth.

2. These are discussion studies. Questions in this guide aim at helping a group discuss together a passage of Scripture in order to understand its content, meaning and implications. Most people are either natural talkers or natural listeners. Yet this type of study works best if people participate more or less evenly. Try to curb any natural tendency to either excessive talking or excessive quiet. You and the rest of the group will benefit.

3. Most questions in this guide allow for a variety of answers. If you disagree with someone else's comment, gently say so. Then explain your own point of view from the passage before you.

4. Be willing to lead a discussion, if asked. Much of the preparation for leading has already been accomplished in the writing of this guide.

5. Respect the privacy of people in your group. Many people speak of things within the context of a Bible study/prayer group that they do not want to be public knowledge. Assume that personal information spoken within the group setting is private, unless you are specifically told otherwise. And don't talk about it elsewhere.

6. We recommend that all groups follow a few basic guidelines and that these guidelines be read at the first session. The guidelines, which you may wish to adapt to your situation, are the following:

   a. Anything said in this group is considered confidential and will not be discussed outside the group unless specific permission is given to do so.

   b. We will provide time for each person present to talk if he or she feels comfortable doing so.

   c. We will talk about ourselves and our own situations, avoiding conversation about other people.

   d. We will listen attentively to each other.

   e. We will pray for each other.

7. Enjoy your study. Prepare to grow. God bless.

Suggestions for Group Leaders

There are specific suggestions to help you in leading in the guidelines for leaders and in the study notes at the back of this guide. Read the guidelines for leaders carefully, even if you are only leading one group meeting. Then you can go to the section on the particular session you will lead.

Introduction: Double Listening

Christians have a reputation for talking too much.

You may remember the elderly Mrs. Moore's experience in the popular book (and movie) *A Passage to India* by E. M. Forster. Inside the famous Marabar Caves, she had experienced the monotonous but terrifying echo—"boum." She had almost fainted. Now outside, she was trying to write a letter. But a strange feeling of despair began to creep over her, when "suddenly, at the edge of her mind, Religion appeared, poor little talkative Christianity, and she knew that all its divine words from 'Let there be light' to 'It is finished' only amounted to 'boum.' "[1]

Needless to say, the words of God are much more substantial than "boum" echoes in a cave, for they are words of truth and of life, which Mrs. Moore did not acknowledge. Nevertheless, the crucial thing is to listen to them with reverent attention and not drown by our own premature talkativeness.

I believe we are called to the difficult and even painful task of "double listening." That is, we are to listen carefully (although, of course, with differing degrees of respect) both to the ancient Word and to the modern world, in order to relate the one to the other with a combination of fidelity and sensitivity. It is my firm conviction that only if we can develop our capacity for double listening will we avoid the opposite pitfalls of unfaithfulness and irrelevance, and be able to speak God's Word to God's world with effectiveness today.

---

[1] E. M. Forster, *A Passage to India* (New York: Penguin, 1985), p. 144.

Study One
The Power of God's Word

Psalm 19:1-11

W
e present you with this Book, the most valuable thing
that this world affords. Here is wisdom; this is the royal law; these
are the lively oracles of God." With these words in the coronation
service the moderator of the General Assembly of the Church of
Scotland handed to the newly crowned Queen Elizabeth a copy
of the Bible.

It might be tempting to dismiss such claims for the Bible as idle
rhetoric, were it not that successive generations of Christian
people have found them to be true. Scripture has brought us light
in darkness, strength in weakness, comfort in sadness. It is not
difficult to endorse the psalmist's experience that the words of
God "are more precious than gold, than much pure gold; they
are sweeter than honey, than honey from the comb" (Psalm
19:10).

Open

☐ What descriptive word did your family use when talking about the Bible?

☐ What words would you use to describe Scripture as you have encountered it? Why?

☐ Describe an experience in which Scripture has helped you or a friend move from pain, or doubt, or fear into assurance of God's love and grace.

Study

Read Psalm 19:1-11:

    [1]The heavens declare the glory of God;
      the skies proclaim the work of his hands.
    [2]Day after day they pour forth speech;
      night after night they display knowledge.
    [3]There is no speech or language
      where their voice is not heard.
    [4]Their voice goes out into all the earth,
      their words to the ends of the world.

    In the heavens he has pitched a tent for the sun,
    [5]which is like a bridegroom coming forth from his pavilion,

like a champion rejoicing to run his course.
⁶It rises at one end of the heavens
    and makes its circuit to the other;
    nothing is hidden from its heat.

⁷The law of the LORD is perfect,
    reviving the soul.
The statutes of the LORD are trustworthy,
    making wise the simple.
⁸The precepts of the LORD are right,
    giving joy to the heart.
The commands of the LORD are radiant,
    giving light to the eyes.
⁹The fear of the LORD is pure,
    enduring forever.
The ordinances of the LORD are sure
    and altogether righteous.
¹⁰They are more precious than gold,
    than much pure gold;
they are sweeter than honey,
    than honey from the comb.
¹¹By them is your servant warned;
    in keeping them there is great reward.

1. What images are suggested by verses 1-6 of this psalm?

2. What do these verses tell us about the nature of God?

3. What synonyms for "the law of the LORD" are given in verses 7-9?

4. What are the words used to describe these synonyms?

5. What do these groupings suggest to you concerning God's Word?

6. In verse 1 the psalmist used the term *God*. Yet in verses 7-11 the more personal term *Lord* is used. What do you think the psalmist is trying to communicate with this distinction?

7. We may find it surprising and odd that the psalmist did not find God's law a burden to him. What do you think enabled the psalmist to see God's laws as "sweeter than honey"?

8. Describe a time when God's law seemed especially appealing or helpful to you.

Commit

☐ Think of someone you know who seems to consistently see God's law as more than just "rules and regulations." What has that person taught you about the power of God's Word?

☐ What concrete ways can you find to see Scripture through the lenses that the psalmist uses?

Ask God to help you to experience the power of his Word in your daily life.

For further reading: Introduction to part three of The Contemporary Christian, *pages 159-60.*

Study Two
Standing in the Word

2 Thessalonians 2:13-17

*T*he people of God must be steadfast. We are summoned to persevere in the truth we have received, to cling to it as a secure handhold in the storm, and to stand firm on this foundation. This is what the New Testament authors have called us to. Hear their voices:

Paul: "So then, brothers, stand firm and hold to the teachings we passed on to you." (2 Thessalonians 2:15)

Hebrews' Author: "We must pay more careful attention, therefore, to what we have heard, so that we do not drift away." (Hebrews 2:1)

John: "See that what you have heard from the beginning remains in you." (1 John 2:24)

Be encouraged that you too can stand in the Word.

Open

☐ How do the teachings of the above authors speak to you?

☐ If you were going to tell someone what effect Scripture could have on his or her life, what would you say?

Study

Read 2 Thessalonians 2:13-17:

[13] But we ought always to thank God for you, brothers loved by the Lord, because from the beginning God chose you to be saved through the sanctifying work of the Spirit and through belief in the truth. [14] He called you to this through our gospel, that you might share in the glory of our Lord Jesus Christ. [15] So then, brothers, stand firm and hold to the teachings we passed on to you, whether by word of mouth or by letter.

[16] May our Lord Jesus Christ himself and God our Father, who loved us and by his grace gave us eternal encouragement and good hope, [17] encourage your hearts and strengthen you in every good deed and word.

1. Verses 13-14 are a marvelously comprehensive statement of God's saving purpose. What actions of God are outlined here?

2. What does the language in verse 15 communicate to you?

What images come to your mind?

3. Paul has just expressed his pleasure about God's work in the Thessalonians. Why does he then command them to "stand firm" and "hold to"?

4. What is it they are to hold on to?

5. Paul is instructing the Thessalonians to hold on to what they have been taught in the context of their Christian fellowship. How does your church help you to stand firm in the teachings of Scripture?

6. How does God encourage our hearts (vv. 16-17)?

7. When do you feel the need to be even more strongly rooted in Scripture?

Commit ————————————————————————

☐ Consider the activities and services you participate in at church. Which of those are helping you to stand firm in the Word?

☐ What could you do to make those opportunities for teaching more fruitful—consider prayer, preparation, study, interaction or application—and to ensure that you are hearing and responding to God's Word?

Thank God for the opportunities you have to grow in the Word, and commit yourself to renewed energy in this area.

For further reading: Chapter ten of The Contemporary Christian, *pages 161-66.*

Study Three
Continuing in the Word

2 Timothy 3:10-17

We are not to be like reeds blown by the wind. We are not to bow down before the prevailing trends of society, its covetousness and materialism, its relativism, and its rejection of all absolute standards of truth and goodness. Instead we are to continue faithfully in the Old and New Testament Scriptures. But why? What is Scripture that it should occupy such an important place in our lives? This study will help you answer those questions.

Open ———————————————————————————
☐ List some of the unhealthy expectations you feel that our society has given to you.

☐ How does society communicate that these things are important?

☐ What resources do you have available to evaluate society's
expectations of you?

Study

Read 2 Timothy 3:10-17:

[10]You, however, know all about my teaching, my way of life,
my purpose, faith, patience, love, endurance, [11]persecutions,
sufferings—what kinds of things happened to me in Antioch,
Iconium and Lystra, the persecutions I endured. Yet the Lord
rescued me from all of them. [12]In fact, everyone who wants to live
a godly life in Christ Jesus will be persecuted, [13]while evil men
and impostors will go from bad to worse, deceiving and being
deceived. [14]But as for you, continue in what you have learned
and have become convinced of, because you know those from
whom you learned it, [15]and how from infancy you have known
the holy Scriptures, which are able to make you wise for salvation
through faith in Christ Jesus. [16]All Scripture is God-breathed and
is useful for teaching, rebuking, correcting and training in
righteousness, [17]so that the man of God may be thoroughly
equipped for every good work.

1. What common thread or threads do you see in Paul's list of personal characteristics (vv. 10-11)?

2. Why was Paul persecuted so regularly?

What is it about the Christian life that compels Paul to say that "every one who wants to live a godly life in Christ Jesus will be persecuted"?

3. What are the things that Timothy had "learned" and "become convinced of" (v. 14)?

4. Paul's admonitions in 14 and 15 are really for all Christians. What are the things that you have "learned and firmly believed"?

When and where do these beliefs come into conflict with the society around you?

5. What does Paul tell Timothy about Scripture in verses 15 and 16?

6. In verse 16 "God-breathed" can also be translated "inspired by God." Why are these two terms so important to our understanding of Scripture?

What difference would it make if we did not know this about the Scriptures?

7. According to verse 17, the purpose of Scripture is "that the man of God may be thoroughly equipped for every good work." How does this contrast with the ways in which Scripture is misused by Christians today?

Commit

☐ Paul called Timothy to stand apart from and against the expectations of his society, even as he lived in that society. In what concrete ways does Paul call you to stand apart from and against the society in which you live?

☐ How can you allow the Scriptures to teach, reprove, correct and train you in your daily life?

Ask God to give you strength and perseverance as you strive to remain true to God's calling in your life.

For further reading: Chapter ten of The Contemporary Christian, *pages 166-72.*

Study Four
Submitting to the Word

John 14:21-24

Submission to the authority of Scripture is *the way of mature discipleship*. A full, balanced and mature life of Christian discipleship is impossible whenever disciples do not submit to their Lord's teaching authority as it is mediated through Scripture.

What is discipleship? It is a many-faceted lifestyle which includes worship, faith, obedience and hope. Every Christian is called to worship God, to trust and obey him, and to look with confident hope toward the future. Yet each of these is a response to revelation, and is seriously impaired without a reliable, objective revelation of God.

Open

☐ Over the years there have been many factors in your Christian growth. Which of the resources listed below have helped you to be a more faithful follower of Christ?

___past traditions of a church ___teachings of your church

___your own reason   ___your own experience

___the witness of a mature   ___sacred/Christian music
   Christian

___devotional writings   ___stirring sermons

☐ How have these helped you?

How have they fallen short?

Study

Read John 14:21-24:

[21] "Whoever has my commands and obeys them, he is the one who loves me. He who loves me will be loved by my Father, and I too will love him and show myself to him."

[22] Then Judas (not Judas Iscariot) said, "But, Lord, why do you intend to show yourself to us and not to the world?"

[23] Jesus replied, "If anyone loves me, he will obey my teaching. My Father will love him, and we will come to him and make our home with him. [24] He who does not love me will not obey my teaching. These words you hear are not my own; they belong to the Father who sent me."

1. The context for this passage is John's version of the Last Supper, as Jesus gave his final thoughts to the disciples. What is

the significance of the setting of this conversation?

2. Imagine that you are one of the disciples at the Last Supper. How would you feel hearing Jesus talk about leaving you and what will happen after he is gone?

3. What promises are made by Jesus in this passage (vv. 16, 18, 21, 23)?

To whom are they addressed?

4. What does Jesus mean when he says, "I will not leave you as orphans; I will come to you" (v. 18)?

5. Several times in this passage Jesus refers to the disciples' being able to see and/or know God. What advantage does this bring to the disciples?

Why does Jesus not intend to show himself to the world in the same way?

6. Mature Christian discipleship is possible only when disciples submit to their Lord's teaching authority as it is mediated through Scripture. How have you seen this to be true in your life?

Commit

☐ When is it difficult to obey the teaching of Scripture?

☐ What does it mean for you to love (obey) Jesus today?

Ask God to become more real to you so that you may better obey his will.

For further reading: Chapter eleven of The Contemporary Christian.

Study Five
Sharing the Word

2 Timothy 1:7-15

David Read writes, "Those of us who enjoy visiting other countries are familiar with that solemn moment when at the frontier we encounter a customs official who . . . fixes us with steely eyes and asks, 'Have you anything to declare?' I have not yet had the nerve to answer, 'Yes, as a minister of the gospel, it is my duty to declare that Jesus Christ is your Lord and Saviour.' " It is lack of conviction about the gospel, he writes, which makes "most of us . . . reluctant evangelists."[1]

There is no chance of the church taking its evangelistic task seriously unless we first recover confidence in the truth, relevance and power of the gospel, and begin to get excited about it again. For this, however, we will have to return to the Bible in which the gospel has been revealed.

Open

☐ In 25 words or (preferably) less, what is the gospel?

☐ On a scale of 1 to 5, rate your willingness to share the gospel with each of the following: a close relative, your boss, your mail carrier, a stranger on an airplane, your best friend and an ex-"significant other."

unlikely		perhaps		likely
1	2	3	4	5

☐ What does this reveal to you about your patterns of evangelism?

Study

Read 2 Timothy 1:7-15:

[7]For God did not give us a spirit of timidity, but a spirit of power, of love and of self-discipline.

[8]So do not be ashamed to testify about our Lord, or ashamed of me his prisoner. But join with me in suffering for the gospel, by the power of God, [9]who has saved us and called us to a holy life—not because of anything we have done but because of his own purpose and grace. This grace was given us in Christ Jesus before the beginning of time, [10]but it has now been revealed through the appearing of our Savior, Christ Jesus, who has

destroyed death and has brought life and immortality to light through the gospel. [11]And of this gospel I was appointed a herald and an apostle and a teacher. [12]That is why I am suffering as I am. Yet I am not ashamed, because I know whom I have believed, and am convinced that he is able to guard what I have entrusted to him for that day.

[13]What you heard from me, keep as the pattern of sound teaching, with faith and love in Christ Jesus. [14]Guard the good deposit that was entrusted to you—guard it with the help of the Holy Spirit who lives in us.

[15]You know that everyone in the province of Asia has deserted me, including Phygelus and Hermogenes.

---

1. Paul is writing his final letter to Timothy, his trusted protégé. What are his concerns in this passage?

---

2. Judging from this passage, what is the gospel (vv. 9-10)?

---

3. Paul seems to be reminding Timothy of not only the power of the gospel but the content as well. When, as Christians, do we need to be reminded of the content of the gospel which we profess?

4. Paul warns Timothy twice about being ashamed. Why do you think this was so important to him?

_____

5. What are the things that make it difficult for you to share the gospel?

_____

6. In verse 12 Paul seems to draw a connection between suffering and being ashamed—that those who suffer should naturally feel shame—and then denies that the connection is valid. In what ways have you experienced the temptation to give in to feeling shame?

_____

7. In verse 12 Paul says that he is not ashamed because "I know whom I have believed . . ." How does this help Paul to strive forward in the proclamation of the gospel?

How does this verse encourage you to proclaim the gospel willingly?

Commit

☐ Think of someone you know who is not living in the power of the gospel as you defined it in question 2. What can you do to help that person?

Pray regularly that God will give you the wisdom to know what others need to hear about the gospel and the courage to say it.

For further reading: Chapter eleven of The Contemporary Christian, *pages 183-85.*

Study Six
Understanding the Word

Isaiah 42:18-25

Before we read the Bible we may sincerely pray, "Please, Lord, I want to see some 'wonderful thing' in your Word."

But he may reply, "What makes you think I have only 'wonderful things' to show you? As a matter of fact, I have some rather *disturbing* things to show you today. Are you prepared to receive them?"

"Oh no, Lord, please do not," we stammer in reply. "I come to Scripture only to be comforted; I really do not want to be challenged or disturbed."

In other words, we come to the Bible with our agenda formulated unilaterally, our expectations preset, our minds made up, laying down in advance what we want God to say to us. Then, instead of hearing the thunderclap of his voice, all we receive is the soothing echoes of our own cultural assumptions.

And God says to us, as he did to his servant through Isaiah: "Hear, you deaf; look and see! Who is blind but my servant, and deaf like the messenger I send?"

Open

☐ What are some of the expectations that we bring when we read the Bible?

Where do these expectations come from?

☐ We all bring cultural assumptions to our reading of the Bible. What cultural assumptions did the biblical authors bring to the Bible?

Study

Read Isaiah 42:18-25:

> [18] "Hear, you deaf;
>   look, you blind, and see!
> [19] Who is blind but my servant,
>   and deaf like the messenger I send?
> Who is blind like the one committed to me,
>   blind like the servant of the LORD?
> [20] You have seen many things, but have paid no attention;
>   your ears are open, but you hear nothing."
> [21] It pleased the LORD

for the sake of his righteousness
to make his law great and glorious.
[22] But this is a people plundered and looted,
all of them trapped in pits
or hidden away in prisons.
They have become plunder,
with no one to rescue them;
they have been made loot,
with no one to say, "Send them back."

[23] Which of you will listen to this
or pay close attention in time to come?
[24] Who handed Jacob over to become loot,
and Israel to the plunderers?
Was it not the LORD,
against whom we have sinned?
For they would not follow his ways;
they did not obey his law.
[25] So he poured out on them his burning anger,
the violence of war.
It enveloped them in flames, yet they did not understand;
it consumed them, but they did not take it to heart.

1. In verses 18-20 God is speaking through Isaiah to the people of Israel. These verses contain several references to hearing and seeing. What point is God trying to make about Israel's ability and willingness to listen?

2. Who is the servant of the Lord?

3. In what way does the servant's blindness and deafness seem different from those addressed in verse 20?

4. Why is Israel "a people plundered and looted" (vv. 24-25)?

5. What was the people's response to God's anger and violence?

6. As children of God, we are susceptible to many of the same dangers that Israel faced. What are some of the ways we are blind to what God desires us to hear and do?

7. When have you wanted to hear something very specific from the Bible?

What did the Bible say to you in those circumstances?

Commit ─────────────────────────────────────
☐ Recognizing our weaknesses is often the first step to overcoming them. Look for specific ways that our culture clouds the way you read the Bible.

Ask God to help you move beyond culture biases as you seek to understand God's will through Scripture, prayer and fellowship.

For further reading: Chapter twelve of The Contemporary Christian.

Guidelines for Leaders

Leading a Bible discussion can be an enjoyable and rewarding experience. But it can also be intimidating—especially if you've never done it before. If this is how you feel, you're in good company.

Remember when God asked Moses to lead the Israelites out of Egypt? Moses replied, "O Lord, please send someone else to do it" (Exodus 4:13). But God gave Moses the help (human and divine) he needed to be a strong leader.

Leading a Bible discussion is not difficult if you follow certain guidelines. You don't need to be an expert on the Bible or a trained teacher. The suggestions listed below can help you to effectively fulfill your role as leader—and enjoy doing it.

Preparing for the Study

1. As you study the passage ahead of time, ask God to help you understand it and apply it in your own life. Unless this happens, you will not be prepared to lead others. Pray too for the various

members of the group. Ask God to open your hearts to the message of his Word and motivate you to action.

2. Read the introduction to the entire guide to get an overview of the subject at hand and the issues which will be explored.

3. Be ready for the "Open" questions with a personal story or example. The group will be only as vulnerable and open as its leader.

4. As you begin preparing for each study, read and reread the assigned Bible passage to familiarize yourself with it. You may want to look up the passage in a Bible so that you can see its context.

5. This study guide is based on the New International Version of the Bible. That is what is reproduced in your guide. It will help you and the group if you use this translation as the basis for your study and discussion.

6. Carefully work through each question in the study. Spend time in meditation and reflection as you consider how to respond.

7. Write your thoughts and responses in the space provided in the study guide. This will help you to express your understanding of the passage clearly.

8. It might help you to have a Bible dictionary handy. Use it to look up any unfamiliar words, names or places. (For additional help on how to study a passage, see chapter five of *Leading Bible Discussions*, IVP.)

9. Take the final (application) questions and the "Commit" portion of each study seriously. Consider what this means for your life, what changes you may need to make in your lifestyle and/or what actions you can take in your church or with people you know. Remember that the group will follow your lead in responding to the studies.

Leading the Study

1. Be sure everyone in your group has a study guide and Bible. Encourage the group to prepare beforehand for each discussion by reading the introduction to the guide and by working through the questions in the study.

2. At the beginning of your first time together, explain that these studies are meant to be discussions, not lectures. Encourage the members of the group to participate. However, do not put pressure on those who may be hesitant to speak during the first few sessions.

3. Begin the study on time. Open with prayer, asking God to help the group understand and apply the passage.

4. Have a group member read the introductory paragraph at the beginning of the discussion. This will remind the group of the topic of the study.

5. Every study begins with a section called *Open*. These "approach" questions are meant to be asked before the passage is read. They are important for several reasons.

First, there is always a stiffness that needs to be overcome before people will begin to talk openly. A good question will break the ice.

Second, most people will have lots of different things going on in their minds (dinner, an exam, an important meeting coming up, how to get the car fixed) that have nothing to do with the study. A creative question will get their attention and draw them into the discussion.

Third, approach questions can reveal where our thoughts or feelings need to be transformed by Scripture. That is why it is especially important not to read the passage before the approach question is asked. The passage will tend to color the honest reactions people would otherwise give, because they feel they are supposed to think the way the Bible does.

6. Have a group member read aloud the passage to be studied.

7. As you ask the questions, keep in mind that they are designed to be used just as they are written. You may simply read them aloud. Or you may prefer to express them in your own words.

There may be times when it is appropriate to deviate from the study guide. For example, a question may already have been answered. If so, move on to the next question. Or someone may raise an important question not covered in the guide. Take time to discuss it, but try to keep the group from going off on tangents.

8. Avoid answering your own questions. Repeat or rephrase them if necessary until they are clearly understood. An eager group quickly becomes passive and silent if members think the leader will give all the *right* answers.

9. Don't be afraid of silence. People may need time to think about the question before formulating their answers.

10. Don't be content with just one answer. Ask, "What do the rest of you think?" or, "Anything else?" until several people have given answers to a question.

11. Acknowledge all contributions. Be affirming whenever possible. Never reject an answer. If it is clearly off-base, ask, "Which verse led you to that conclusion?" or, "What do the rest of you think?"

12. Don't expect every answer to be addressed to you, even though this will probably happen at first. As group members become more at ease, they will begin to truly interact with each other. This is one sign of healthy discussion.

13. Don't be afraid of controversy. It can be stimulating! If you don't resolve an issue completely, don't be frustrated. Move

on and keep it in mind for later. A subsequent study may solve
the problem.

14. Periodically summarize what the group has said about the
passage. This helps to draw together the various ideas mentioned
and gives continuity to the study. But don't preach.

15. Don't skip over the application questions at the end of
each study. It's important that we each apply the message of the
passage to ourselves in a specific way. Be willing to get things
started by describing how you have been affected by the study.

Depending on the makeup of your group and the length of time
you've been together, you may or may not want to discuss the
"Commit" section. If not, allow the group to read it and reflect
on it silently. Encourage members to make specific commitments
and to write them in their study guide. Ask them the following
week how they did with their commitments.

16. Conclude your time together with conversational prayer.
Ask for God's help in following through on the commitments
you've made.

17. End on time.

Many more suggestions and helps are found in *The Big Book
on Small Groups, Small Group Leaders' Handbook* and *Good
Things Come in Small Groups* (IVP). Reading through one of
these books would be worth your time.

Study Notes

Study 1. The Power of God's Word. Psalm 19:1-11.

Purpose: To explore the power of God's Word to play a positive role in our lives.

Question 1. One of God's methods of self-revelation is general revelation, through the glory of nature, especially in the heavens (as in these verses). These verses show three aspects of this revelation: it is continuous (v. 2), abundant and universal. This knowledge of God is available to all people (see Romans 10:18).

Question 2. These verses employ a common characteristic of Hebrew poetry, parallelism—the use of similar words and phrases to give emphasis to an image or picture. The various synonyms of *law*—*statutes, precepts, commands, fear* and *ordinances*—are used to show the rich and varied nature of God's self-revelation in the Torah. This revelation is more specific than what was offered in verses 1-6. As Christians, we really read the series of synonyms as referring to all of God's word in Scripture.

One particular word in the series of synonyms does not seem to fit as well—*fear* of the Lord. Some scholars translate it as *word* of the Lord. However, it could also be seen that "fear of the Lord" is used to emphasize that the point of God's self-disclosure is a humble and reverent worship of God.

Question 5. One clue might be that each time the psalmist describes the law he unfolds its beneficial effects—for example, reviving the soul (v. 7). Another advantage the psalmist had was the ability to see that God's law, or God's Word, was really God's way of showing us what he is like.

Question 6. The Hebrew word for "God" used in the first verse of the psalm is *El*, emphasizing the "God of Creation." However, the word used in verses 7-11 is *Yahweh*, emphasizing the "God of the Covenant." This "God of the Covenant" is a more personal being, whose very will can be known by his people.

Question 7. Such a perspective seems to assume that a person understands God's love, and that God's law is given to protect us and to make our lives more stable and healthy.

Study 2. Standing in the Word. 2 Thessalonians 2:13-17.
Purpose: To discover how Scripture can provide a strong basis for our lives.

Question 1. The apostle alludes to the three persons of the Trinity, and in particular makes two parallel affirmations. The basic statements are as follows:

2:13 God chose you from the beginning to be saved through the sanctification of the Spirit.

2:14 God called you through the gospel to share in Christ's glory.

Question 2. The apostle's exhortation is a double one: "Stand firm!" and "hold to!" He seems to picture a gale, in which they are in danger both of being swept off their feet and of being wrenched from their handhold. In face of this hurricane-force wind, he urges them to stand their ground, planting their feet firmly on *terra firma*, and to cling to something solid and secure, clutching hold of it for dear life. Both verbs are present imperatives. Since the storm may rage for a long time, they must keep on standing firm and keep on holding fast.

Question 3. We need to absorb the apostle's unexpected logic. For we would probably have drawn a different conclusion from what he has just written. We might have said: "We are bound to give thanks for you . . . because God chose you . . . and God called you to share in Christ's eternal glory. So then, brothers, relax and take it easy!" But Paul's appeal is the opposite. Far from relaxing, they must brace themselves. Far from lying down and falling asleep, they must stand firm. That is, Paul's assurance regarding God's steadfast purpose for his people, instead of justifying irresponsible slackness, is the very basis on which he can urge them with confidence to be steadfast themselves.

Question 4. What they are to hold onto is specified. It is *the teachings* (*paradoseis*, "traditions"). *Paradosis* means truth which, having been received, must be faithfully handed on. In this case it is Paul's own teaching, which he had received from God (cf. 1 Thessalonians 2:13) and which subsequently, he writes, *we passed on to you, whether by word of mouth* (his oral instruction when present with them) *or by letter* (his written instruction when absent). So these *paradoseis* are not the later traditions of the church, but the original teachings or traditions of the apostles. It is vital to preserve this distinction between the two kinds of tradition. The apostolic traditions are the foundation of Christian faith and life, while subsequent ecclesiastical traditions are the superstructure which the church has erected on it. The primary traditions, to which we should hold fast, are those which the apostles received from Christ (either the historic Christ or the living Spirit of Christ), which they taught the early church by word or letter, and which are now preserved in the New Testament.

To "stand firm and hold to the teachings" means in our case to be biblical or evangelical Christians, to be uncompromisingly loyal to the teaching of Christ and his apostles. This is the road to stability. The only way to resist false teaching is to cling to the true teaching.

Question 5. Paul's appeal for stability is made to the Thessalonians as *brothers* (v. 15). This is a recognition that the context within which they were to "stand firm and hold to the teachings" was the Christian fellowship, the family of God. In other words, we need each other. The church is the fellowship of faith, the society for sacred study. In it we receive teaching from pastors who are duly authorized to expound the tradition of the apostles, we wrestle together with its contemporary application, and we teach and admonish each other out of the same Scriptures. It is the Bible in the church which can develop our Christian stability and so strengthen us to withstand the pressures of persecution, false teaching and temptation.

Study 3. Continuing in the Word. 2 Timothy 3:10-17.
Purpose: To discover the importance of Scripture in the way we live our lives.
Question 1. There are at least two important things to notice about the list. The first is to read this list as a response to Paul's earlier remarks about the godless people in 3:1-5. The contrast with the first paragraph of this chapter is obvious. The men described there were following their own inclinations (they were lovers of self, money and pleasure), and their pathetic converts had been carried away by their own impulses. Timothy, on the

other hand, has followed an altogether different standard, namely the teaching and the example of Christ's apostle, Paul. So Paul goes on to list the characteristics of his life, in contrast to that of the self-lovers whom he has characterized in verses 2-5. The other thing to notice is that the list consists of Paul's actions toward others. Each of the items in the list centers around Paul's desire and efforts to minister to others in the name of Christ. This is to be Timothy's model, and the basis for Timothy's trust in Paul's admonitions.

Question 2. There were various specific reasons for each of Paul's individual persecutions. In fact, some of Paul's experiences that we would count as persecutions were really self-induced. The incidents Paul refers to in this passage are narrated at length in Acts 13:14—14:23.

Whatever the specifics of a particular persecution, it was invariably Paul's message, coupled with the witness of his life, that got him in trouble. In instructing Timothy to follow his example, Paul calls Timothy to be different from the world around him, to resist the mood of the world, and to stand firm against it. Paul's persecutions were proof that the low standards of the world were irreconcilable with Paul's own teaching and conduct.

The implication for us, then, is that as Christians we should speak and act in such a way that our values and behavior cause the surrounding culture to recognize its own bankruptcy.

Question 3. The content of what Timothy has learned and "become convinced of" is directly connected to how he has learned. These teachers from whom Timothy had learned are probably, first, his mother and grandmother who had taught him the Old Testament from his infancy (v. 15, cf. 1:5) and, second, the apostle, whose "teaching" (v. 10) Timothy knew and which is preserved in the New Testament. These teachers of Timothy are contrasted with the evil men and impostors whose false teaching Paul considered so dangerous.

We know that Timothy was well versed in the Old Testament Scriptures through the efforts of his mother and grandmother. However, we can also assume that Timothy had become convinced about Paul and/or Peter's teaching about Jesus as the Messiah and Savior.

Question 4. For some people this includes the traditions and belief systems of a Christian family. For others it means a more recent set of beliefs and values.

Question 5. Paul tells Timothy three things: Scripture is able to instruct toward salvation—for this reason Jesus Christ is himself the center of the biblical revelation. Scripture is God-breathed— it is God's Word for humanity. Scripture is useful—it is essential for our growth into maturity in Christ.

Question 6. The phrase *God-breathed* indicates that Scripture is the Word of God, spoken by God, or breathed out of the mouth of God. However, when God spoke, he did not speak into space. Human authors, even while God was speaking to and through them, were themselves actively engaged in historical research, theological reflection and literary composition. Thus on the one hand God spoke, determining what he wanted to say, yet without smothering the personality of the human authors. On the other hand, human beings spoke, using their faculties freely, yet without distorting the truth which God was speaking through them.

Because of this duality, it is important to be conscious of how we read the Bible. Because Scripture is the Word of God, we should read it as we read no other book—on our knees, humbly, looking to the Spirit for inspiration. Because Scripture is also the words of human beings, we should read it as every other book, using our minds.

Question 7. All too often Scripture is seen not as a gift from God to lead us into greater understanding of our Creator, but rather as a personal tool to impose a certain set of desires onto others. But Scripture is nobody's private possession; it is public property. Having been given by God, it belongs to all.

Study 4. Submitting to the Word. John 14:21-24.

Purpose: To understand how our obedience to Jesus allows us to see God more clearly.

Question 1. Note the first two verses of chapter 13: "It was just before the Passover Feast. Jesus knew that the time had come for him to leave this world and go to the Father. Having loved his own who were in the world, he now showed them the full extent of his love. The evening meal was being served, and the devil had already prompted Judas Iscariot, son of Simon, to betray Jesus."

The passage studied here is part of the conversation where Jesus "showed them the full extent of his love." In a sense Jesus is giving the disciples their "marching orders."

In verses 21-24 Jesus appears to be speaking more specifically about the disciples, and not the rest of the world. By extension, then, Jesus is also speaking to the church today.

Question 3. All of the promises seemed to be addressed to those who love Jesus and do what he commands, first the disciples, and then by implication us.

Question 4. Jesus is looking forward to a time when he would no longer be with the disciples in the same way. Instead, he is

anticipating the coming of the Holy Spirit, who will come in Jesus'
name (see 14:26). Jesus is encouraging the disciples just before
their time of greatest sorrow.

Study 5. Sharing the Gospel. 2 Timothy 1:7-15.

Purpose: To gain courage to share the gospel by exploring its
meaning.

Question 1. Paul has both specific and general concerns as he
writes this letter. Throughout the letter he makes specific references to Timothy's weaknesses or "growing edges." These things
tell us much about Timothy, and that God can use people who
are not perfect.

Paul also gives more general instructions, things that are more
universal. These are also directed to Timothy, but are equally
important for us to hear. In this passage they revolve around the
idea and content of the gospel, which Paul is very concerned
about, especially as he realizes his days as an evangelist are
numbered. He desperately wants to see Timothy, and those like
him, carry on the work of spreading the gospel.

Question 2. In verses 9 and 10 Paul communicates three aspects
of the gospel: the character of salvation—that "God saved us,"
"called us to a holy life" and "brought life and immortality to
light through the gospel." Salvation in this passage in the comprehensive purpose of God by which he justifies, sanctifies and
glorifies his people.

The second aspect of salvation is its source—this source is
God's purpose and grace, which was given to us in Christ Jesus
before the beginning of time. Our own efforts do not figure into
the equation at all.

The third aspect is the ground of salvation—the ground of

salvation is the historical work of Christ in the Incarnation, in which Christ destroyed death, releasing us from its power; the other side of this is that Christ brought life and immortality. This is an especially strong statement, considering Paul was in the process of dealing with his own imminent death. But Paul is certainly speaking of the ultimate destruction of death, which has not yet been fully realized.

Question 4. The issue of being ashamed of the gospel is a common concern of Paul's. However, this concern has been intensified because of some setbacks that Paul has seen in the recent past, summarized in verse 15 with "everyone in the province . . . has deserted me." As an old man looking back on his life's work, it is only natural that Paul be especially sensitive to the possibility of his work and teaching's being abandoned by his trusted friends.

Question 7. This verse can be translated in two different ways. The traditional translation emphasizes the assurance of personal salvation, as Paul expresses his faith that God is able to protect Paul's faith in Jesus Christ until it is most needed.

However, "what I have entrusted to him" could be translated "my deposit." This would mean that Paul had faith that God could protect the deposit given to Paul (the gospel), even beyond Paul's failings. This is based on Paul's knowledge of God.

This would have been a real encouragement to Timothy also, as he was no doubt nervous about carrying on Paul's legacy. And it should also be an encouragement to us. Ultimately, it is God himself who is the guarantor of the gospel. It is his responsibility to preserve it. We must play our part in guarding and defending the truth. Nevertheless, in entrusting the deposit to our hands, he has not taken his own hands off it.

Study 6. Understanding the Word. Isaiah 42:18-25.

Purpose: To recognize the barriers that exist when we read Scripture so that we may move beyond our limitations to hear God speak.

Open. These opening questions may open up a new line of thinking for some members of the group. Cultural prejudices can be subtle, and we may easily think we are free of them. However, when we are not aware of our assumptions, we may be deceived into believing that what we see in the Bible is the only thing to be seen.

In its long history, the church has seldom been sensitively in tune with God's Word. More often it has been conformist, as Paul warned in Romans 12:2. This conforming to the needs and expectations of society can be seen in the Christian backing of the Crusades, religious wars in Europe, slavery, Nazism, economic disparity and the arms race. Each of these evils was perpetuated by Christians who went to the Bible with an agenda and managed to verify that agenda by the use of Scripture.

Question 1. One important point in these verses is that the people of Israel do not hear God at least in part because they are not willing to make the effort, especially in verse 20. Although God originally spoke to Israel in these verses, it is important for us to hear the same message. Listening to God is not a passive endeavor, but one that requires us to actively seek out the meaning beneath the surface.

Question 2. "Scholars hold differing views of the identity of the Servant. . . . The servant is the nation . . . an individual . . . or both" (Bruce Metzger and Roland E. Murphy, eds., *The New Oxford Annotated Bible* [New York: Oxford University Press, 1991], p. 922). In this particular passage, the precise identity is not crucial; however, it does seem that the servant is not precisely identified with the entire nation of Israel.

Question 3. It may be that God does not see blindness as essentially the problem. Note that in verse 16 of this chapter God promises to lead the blind himself. Yet those who are blind in verse 20 are unwilling to see, so God cannot help them.

Question 4. While this prophecy refers to a particular event in the life of Israel, it follows a cyclical pattern established much earlier in the relationship between Yahweh and his people. The people in their blindness have refused to follow and obey God, and God has punished them. This cycle is completed in Israel's rescue by God. "Jacob" is a reference to the people of Israel.

Question 5. The image of the people of Israel after God's wrath seems to be of someone who is oblivious to the severity of the situation around them, someone who is beyond caring. Yet in chapter 43 God nonetheless promises to rescue and redeem Israel.

Christian Basics Bible Studies from InterVarsity Press

Christian Basics are the keys to becoming a mature disciple. The studies in these guides, based on material from some well-loved books, will take you through key Scripture passages and help you to apply biblical truths to your life. Each guide has six studies for individuals or groups.

Character: Who You Are When No One's Looking by Bill Hybels. We all do our best when others are watching. But what about when no one is looking? That's where character comes in, giving us consistency when it's just between God and us.

Courage. Discipline. Vision. Endurance. Compassion. Self-sacrifice. The qualities covered in this Bible study guide provide a foundation for character. With this foundation and God's guidance, we can maintain character even when we face temptations and troubles.

Christ: Basic Christianity by John Stott. God himself is seeking us. Through his Son, Jesus Christ, God wants to offer us his love.

But who is this Jesus Christ? These studies explore the person and character of this man who has altered the face of history.

Come, and discover him for the first time or in a new and deeper way.

Commitment: My Heart—Christ's Home by Robert Boyd Munger. What would it be like to have Christ come into the home of our hearts? Moving from room to room with him, we discover what he desires for us. Are we prepared to meet with him daily in our living room? in our recreation room? in the study? What about that dark closet that needs cleaning out?

These studies will take you through six of the rooms of your heart, helping you to see aspects of your Christian life as Jesus sees them. You will be stretched and enriched by your personal meetings with Christ in each study.

Prayer: Too Busy Not to Pray by Bill Hybels. Most of us have trouble finding time to pray. There's so much going on—work, church, school, family, relationships: the list is never-ending. Someone always seems to need something from us. But time for God, time to pray, seems impossible to find.

These studies are designed to help you slow down and listen to God. But they don't stop there! They also help you to learn how to respond. As a result, you will grow closer to God and experience the benefits of spending time with him.

Priorities: Tyranny of the Urgent by Charles Hummel. Have you ever wished for a thirty-hour day? Every week we leave a trail of unfinished tasks. Unanswered letters, unvisited friends and unread books haunt our waking moments. We desperately need relief.

These studies are designed to help you put your life back in order by discovering what is *really* important. Find out what God's priorities are for you.

Scripture: God's Word for Contemporary Christians by John Stott. What is the place of Scripture in our lives? We know it is important—God's Word to us—but how can it make a difference to us each day?

In this guide, John Stott will show you the power Scripture can have in your life. These studies will help you make the Bible your anchor to God in the face of the temptation and corruption that are all around.

Work: Serving God by What We Do by Ben Patterson. "I can serve God in church, but can I serve him on the job?" In the factory, in the office, in the home, on the road, on the farm—Ben Patterson says we can give glory to God wherever he calls us.

Work, even what seems to us the most mundane, is what God created us for. He is our employer. These studies will show you how your work can become meaningful and satisfying.

Worship: Serving God with Our Praise by Ben Patterson. Our deepest need can be filled only as we come to our Creator in worship. This is the divine drama in which we are all invited to participate, not as observers but as performers. True worship will transform every part of our lives, and these studies will help you to understand and experience the glory of praising God.